How to Start [A Fire]

In a Survival [Situation]

Survival and Prepping Series

M. Usman

Mendon Cottage Books

JD-Biz Publishing

All Rights Reserved.

No part of this publication may be reproduced in any form or by any means, including scanning, photocopying, or otherwise without prior written permission from JD-Biz Corp Copyright © 2015

All Images Licensed by Fotolia and 123RF.

Disclaimer

The information is this book is provided for informational purposes only. It is not intended to be used and medical advice or a substitute for proper medical treatment by a qualified health care provider. The information is believed to be accurate as presented based on research by the author.

The contents have not been evaluated by the U.S. Food and Drug Administration or any other Government or Health Organization and the contents in this book are not to be used to treat cure or prevent disease.

The author or publisher is not responsible for the use or safety of any diet, procedure or treatment mentioned in this book. The author or publisher is not responsible for errors or omissions that may exist.

Warning

The Book is for informational purposes only and before taking on any diet, treatment or medical procedure, it is recommended to consult with your primary health care provider.

Our books are available at

1. Amazon.com
2. Barnes and Noble
3. Itunes
4. Kobo
5. Smashwords
6. Google Play Books

Table of Contents

Chapter 1 – Introduction 4
   1.1 Importance of Fire 4
   1.2 Fire for Survival 5
   1.3 Methods of Starting Fire 6
Chapter 2 – Friction Based Fire 9
   2.1 Hand Drill 9
   2.2 Bow Drill 10
   2.3 Stone and Steel 12
Chapter 3 – Starting Fire with Batteries 14
   3.1 Battery and Steel Wool 14
   3.2 Fire in the Gum Wrapper 15
Chapter 4 – Fire from Lenses 16
   4.1 Conventional Lenses 16
   4.2 Unconventional Lenses 17
Chapter 5 – Ready to use Methods 19
   5.1 Magnesium Strip 19
   5.2 Survival Bracelets 20
Chapter 6 – Things to Remember 22
   6.1 Fire bed and its location 22
   6.2 Tinder 23
   6.3 Fuel 23
   6.4 Safety 24
Conclusion 25
Author Bio 26
Publisher 37

Chapter 1 – Introduction

1.1 Importance of Fire

Have you ever thought about what you would have done to boil your breakfast egg if you were born a couple of million years ago? There were hundreds of ways which were used to make fire out of almost nowhere, and they fulfilled some of those elementary purposes for which fire is used, even today. We are least likely to come across situations and circumstances that our stone-aged ancestors faced, where they were required to make fire to survive. Nevertheless, the tools and technologies that today's sophisticated and highly advanced world has brought to us are useful only when they are within access. You will need knowledge, skills, educated ideas, and some basic tools to start a fire when you are stuck in a far-flung island all by yourself. All you need is a tall flame to make yourself noticed and be located. You will need these skills when you are staying overnight in a zone you chose to chase game if you forget to bring matches or a lighter to start fire, which could keep you warm and prevent wild animals from coming near.

The link between man and fire traces back to the ages when one of the very first human creatures, or something close to that, landed on this earth. This primal relationship between human and fire highlights the importance of fire and how pivotal a role its existence plays in our survival. From cooking to heating and from signaling to repelling predators, fire has been one of the primary ingredients of the basic human survival toolkit. Interestingly, the mythological and spiritual part of fire in various religions or cults of the world also dates back to primitive ages. It can also be assumed that men understood fire and its utility in different ways, which mainly evolved from their experiences with it. Thanks to our ancestors who developed the ability to use fire in several ways and transferred this ability, each generation has only added more value to the application of fire. Without knowing about anthropology, one can safely say that this skill required memory, analysis, and future planning – the traits that separated us from our earliest ancestors. Since then, fire has done nothing but facilitated us and provided us with an easier life. For example, generating the power that runs my PC, heating your home, or running some artillery that protects us are ways we enjoy an easier life. The more sophisticated and advanced form of fire utility, like industrial or military use, brings a plethora of advantages and disadvantages on the table to debate about. However, we shall focus on some of the most commonly used and essential applications of fire such as methods of setting up fire with limited quirky tools in unseen situations.

1.2 Fire for Survival

Survival skills should be learned with rhymes as the situation warranting these skills can come at any time and age. Having possession of these skills with some common sense can help one sustain unscathed for long periods or until some help approaches. It can even help to get out of such situations, no matter how dangerous or prolonged they may seem. Survival skills comprise of techniques and methods which may be used to produce, avail, or access the necessities that are mandatory for human survival, including but not limited to water, food, first aid, navigation, shelter, and fire. Unquestionably, being conscious and in the right frame of mind as well as the ability to think straight in such situations is a prerequisite in order to be capable of using the survival methods to stay afloat for the maximum possible time or until a human aid arrives. Emergency is unseen and sometimes comes with added adversaries. That means one is never prepared enough to cater to a condition which calls for having survival skills.

Amongst several of these skills and objects required for survival, fire is one of the most important and has the highest utility in endurance tests. The existence of fire drastically increases chances of survival and it is also deemed as a secondary source of boosting physical and mental stability in volatile and dangerous conditions. The fire satisfies many survival needs including producing light, providing warmth, cooking/disinfecting food, boiling water, resisting predators, aiding navigation, drying clothes, making signals, etc. The importance and use of fire has been discussed in numerous books, articles, and other literary works and a special stress has been placed on fire making skills before venturing into activities or projects that may bring you in the middle of harsh conditions. Fire can be a central point and even a metaphoric source of protection and energy at times which are otherwise difficult in the wilderness.

1.3 Methods of Starting Fire

As discussed in earlier parts of this book, fire can aid drastically in staying safe unless you are rescued from an emergency or life threatening situation. However, it is not easy to master this craft at setting up fire through unconventional methods. It not only requires specific skills, techniques, and tools, but also needs plenty of time, patience, and presence of mind.

Whether you require melting snow for drinking water or adventure overnight by starting a camp fire, it is not possible without having the right type of skills and maybe some practice. Before camping or ambitiously accepting a challenging task, make sure that you have right skills and tools to start and utilize the benefits of fire.

There are several methods with some based on technology and some based on simple physics. We will also learn about some methods which use natural resources like wind and sun-heat to start fire and convert it into flames.

Unbelievable though it may sound, fire can even start from water and ice with right kind of skills and techniques. Selection of the right method hinges upon the following factors that should be considered precisely before starting the effort.

1. Atmosphere: Certain methods are pertinent and fruitful in dry and warm atmospheres only, while some methods are workable in wet conditions. While evaluating the choices of methods available in a situation that is deemed difficult to manage, one should always include weather and atmosphere for making the right decision.

2. Physical Condition: One might be drained out in survival situation already and not able to consume the energy and endurance required to start fire through specific methods. In such cases, it is better to select methods which do not require much physical exertion and energy.

3. Surroundings: By surroundings we mean what is around you when you start feeling that your survival is endangered. Is it a wild animal attacking immediately? Or are you are stuck in a deep forest and have you're your navigation? Different methods suit different conditions and therefore the technique used in the middle of the sea while floating on a static boat might not come handy when you need to cook your next meal on the course of a mountain track.

4. Access to Material: Access to required material is key to success. Availability and application of these tools and materials depends upon your surrounding and your proximity to these tools. When on a mountain climbing mission, you may find stone and metals closer to you than wood and trees.

5. Time: It is very crucial to assess how much time is available to you before you can manage without fire. Time is again assessed in parallel with situation and surrounding and it is pivotal. This is because some methods may require as much as 30 to 60 minutes before you start reaping benefits of fire that are required as per the survival situation.

In the following chapters we shall explain in detail a few easy-to-use but unconventional methods of starting fire. Remember that the list is not limited to these skills or methods and one should always explore and chose from the most dependable, safe, and easy to apply methods before going into the wilderness.

Chapter 2 – Friction Based Fire

Fire created from friction is probably one of the most ancient and most commonly used emergency methods to start and use fire. It is based on simple physics and requires exactly the same science that you have seen in Hollywood movies when a car without tires drag alongside the road and the metal rims collide with concrete resulting in fire sparks and flames. Exuberance, tireless hands, absolute dry wood, pieces of cloth, stone, and steel are few of the most important ingredients for this method to be successful depending upon what you chose to apply. It is helpful to share a few basic facts about friction based methods before we jump to the mechanics of the methods.

1. All friction based methods are used in extremely dry atmospheres. Precipitation, snow, and highly humid environments are not congenial at all for friction based methods.

2. It is good to keep a few pieces of dry wood, steel, and stone handy while venturing into tough terrains, as you may not have enough time or you might not find all the tools when required.

3. Warning: The below detailed friction methods are applied manually with direct involvement of hands, so there are high chances of cuts, bruises, and burns. Use the methods neatly and very carefully to assure your hands are placed off from striking materials and sparks coming out at them.

Let's have look at some friction based methods:

2.1 Hand Drill

Aspen, cottonwood, willow, walnut, and cypress are perfect wood fuel as long as they are perfectly dry. Get hold of a dry wood board that is as flat as it possibly can be. All we need here is this board and a stick like a spindle which needs to be grinded inside a depressed cup like area that we are going to create in the wood board.

Step 1: Create a cut on the board in a shape that looks like a 'V'. Then create a small depression adjacent to the cut that should be preferably in a round or oval shape. The depression may not be deep, but it should be in a shape good enough to fix the spindle firmly inside it so it doesn't slip. You will need a sharp edged tool to create this depression and one can always put a small amount of tinder or dry bush beneath this depression so it can easily catch fire.

Step 2: Insert the tip of spindle in the depression and start rolling it between your palms. The height of the spindle is also important as the rolling of the spindle is an exhorting job that should be done while sitting in a comfortable position. Roll your palms at a very quick speed until you start seeing an ember around the tip of the spindle that is rolling inside the depression.

Step 3: It should have already been 20-40 minutes of continuous grinding until the spindle starts getting red and you get a hint of smoke, ash, or ember near its end. Transfer the ember to tinder, dry bush, or kindle that you have collected to use as fuel and protect it until a flame is ignited.

2.2 Bow Drill

This is the most efficient and easy to apply friction method which has evolved in this form from manual hand based drilling. You will need all tools required for a hand drill apart from a flexible but strong string and a small softwood club like stick to create a bow. This is a semi-automated version of hand drill.

Step 1: The main fire board is formed in same way as in the case of the hand drill and the hole or depression is created alongside a cut at the edge. The spindle is fixed inside this hole tightly so that it strikes with the walls of the board when pressure is applied and the spindle stick is rolled with speed.

Step 2: Create a socket with soft wood which fixes the either side of the spindle inside it. This is what you use as a handle to hold the bow and push down to apply pressure with one hand. The other hand is used to swing the bow which fixes the spindle that rolls inside the board to build the ember.

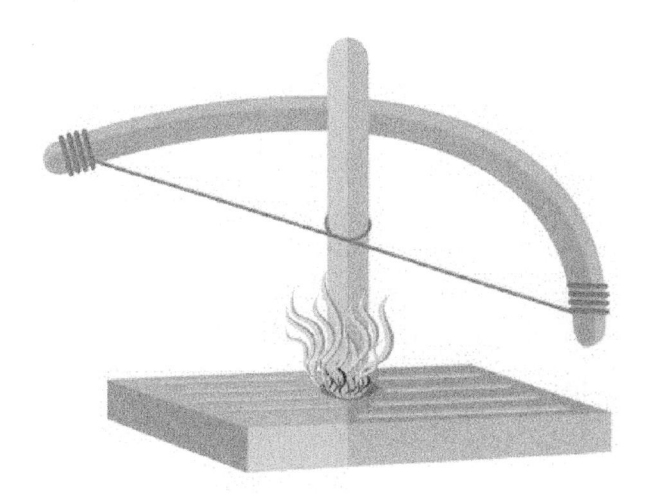

Step 3: Create a bow with softwood that can curve or a naturally curved stick with a length equivalent to the length of your arm. A lace of rubber, shoelace, or rope that doesn't break can be the perfect choice for making the string of the bow. Tie the spindle in the bow string in a loop and fix or tie it on both sides of the stick to form a bow.

Step 4: Start whirling your bow back and forth quickly while holding your spindle's top with the socket. This bow based method works as a mechanical rotation drill and is used in place of a hand drill as seen in picture above.

2.3 Stone and Steel

This is an old fashioned and classic style of starting fire in the absence of matches or a lighter. Unlike drilling methods this technique is simple, easy, and may require lesser exertion as compared to drilling methods. To apply this method of starting fire, you will need a flint stone and a piece of steel to strike each other and char cloth to catch fire.

Step 1: Take a flint like rock piece of a size that you can easily grip in your fist. A flint that is perfect for applying this method would have a sharp edge that can strike a steel surface well and produce friction. If one cannot find a flint with an edge then the edge should be carved with another stone or metal.

Step 2: The steel used in this method is high carbon that is hard enough to create resisting friction when rubbed with the flint. Remember, it is the steel which creates sparks and ignites so better not wear it out while rubbing or you will have to start all over. Try having a chunk of steel which looks like the letter "C".

Step 3: It is the char cloth that is your fuel in this fashion. A char cloth is cotton or linen that is cooked in a closed environment without much of a supply of oxygen. You can put a small piece of linen cloth or cotton pieces in a holed tin can or metal bottle and cook them in fire for 15-20 minutes to get char cloth.

Step 4: Wrap the flint with char cloth in a way that it partially exposes the edged surface of stone, to strike steel on it. The objective is to shave off steel dust with friction that will be hot enough to convert into fire spark. Once it lands on the char cloth it will start glowing or forming a crescent.

Step 5: As soon as the char cloth starts glowing, blow on it until you see the spark spreading. Place this glowing smoky cloth on the tinder or bush bed that you have already prepared and keep blowing until you see fire catching the tinder and making a flame.

Chapter 3 – Starting Fire with Batteries

Creating survival fire is not as much of a tedious and cumbersome mission with batteries as it seems with help of other techniques. Batteries are commonly used sources of electric power and energy and they are equally good when it comes to sparking fire in the wildwoods. Batteries contain electrolyte, anode, and cathode and have two different source points; a positive and a negative.

If you are in a situation where you deem fire as something that can give you a new life and you are in possession of somewhat charged batteries and pieces of conductor metal then do not worry. You have got everything to be lucky. Almost every type of metal, which is a good conductor, works with batteries to start fire when brought in the right of kind contact.

3.1 Battery and Steel Wool

This method works with 9V battery sizes since its negative and positive terminals are on the same side. Take the steel wool in one hand in a way that sparks generated on it do not hurt or burn your fingers. Make sure that your tinder is close to the location where you are applying this method as the sparks may not last very long.

Step 1: Make sure that the steel wool is handled strong as a condensed metal ball, as this way you will have more metal to create sparks.

Step 2: Find a battery that has two terminals on the same side such as a 9V battery. Terminals are two nodes or prongs that are mostly circular in shape.

Step 3: Rub the battery on the steel wool as rapidly as you can in a fashion that both the terminals strike with the metal wool at the same time hence creating current in the metal. You will soon see sparking between the tiny steel wires that will grow to form crimson kindle.

Step 4: Keep blowing the kindle while placing it in the middle of the tinder at the same time. Do not stop blowing unless tinder catches fire.

3.2 Fire in the Gum Wrapper

If you are fond of chewing gum, this method can help you. Alternatively, any metal or even semi-metal filament can be used to ignite fire through this method by bringing the metal string in contact with AA or AAA sized batteries in the perfect way.

Step 1: Get hold of a gum wrapper that is preferably a foil strip which comes in moldable hard material. Cut a long narrow strip from the foil that is 1/4" in width of the original size of the wrapper.

Step 2: Fold this narrow strip exactly from the middle so that foil side of the strip is faced downward. The strip can catch fire from anywhere, so make sure that the center of the strip is a little elevated from the two corners.

Step 3: Fold the quarters of the strip from both ends to form brackets. Now, touch these brackets parallel on both terminals of the battery. The strip will catch fire in no time after which you can transfer the strip to your tinder bundle.

Chapter 4 – Fire from Lenses

This is one of the modern methods in this book, just like the ones based on batteries. The modern methods are based on modern sciences while the primitive methods like friction ones are based on basic physics. Hence, the modern methods need less mechanical workaround and friction based methods need more exertion.

The lens here doesn't exactly mean the magnifying glass or concave lenses made out of glass or mirrors. This can be any material which can perform the job of creating a required reflex from sunlight that is needed to light fire. Of course, these methods are workable on sunny days only.

4.1 Conventional Lenses

Magnifying glasses, inverted mirrors, lenses of eyeglasses, or binoculars are ideal objects to create intensified spotlight aimed at a point on tinder, since they have short focal length. This method cannot be used in the overcast conditions or in the night, but is very effective and quick to apply otherwise.

Step 1: You can choose your lenses from the list of choices available to you with convenience. Your main object is purported lenses that create a direct beam of magnified sunlight.

Step 2: A beam can be created by placing the lenses in a way in which the angle of the lenses is towards the sun and a direct sunlight beam is pointed towards the tinder bundle.

The intensified spot is reflected by a small circle of bright light on your tinder – this is your focal area. Keep movement of your hand to a minimum if you are carrying the lenses to ensure maximum heat to the point before you get fire. Try and adjust the lenses to focus the tinder with the light circle as small as possible; the smaller the focal area, the hotter the focal point becomes. Also remember that if you are using spectacles or binoculars, always use them inverted as to the normal usage when using them to start an emergency fire. The bigger side of binoculars should face the sun and the eye-set should face the tinder to create an intensified hot spot on the tinder. Similarly, in order to create fire, the spectacles should be used by facing the external side, which is usually convex in shape, towards the sun.

4.2 Unconventional Lenses

You can use interesting stuff like balloons, condoms, or even ice as an alternative to lenses used in binoculars or glasses. The angular placement and concentration of the focal point is crucial in cases where unconventional lenses are used. Successful application of any of these unconventional or mechanical methods described in this book, require extensive prior practice.

Step 1: Fill the condom or balloon with water and make it as much round as possible by tying one end tightly. Trust your judgment and do not inflate it too much or it will disperse the sunlight.

Step 2: Squeeze the balloon or condom from the middle to form two spherical halves that will give you two circular light spots on the tinder. As both balloons and condoms have short focal lengths, select the part that produces a smaller and more intensified spot on the tinder and focus on that until it ignites the tinder.

An ice block can also be used in the same manner and it works just like a magnifying glass when carved into a lens like shape.

Step 1: Take a clear ice block that is at least 2 inches thick and free of haze or impurities inside. If any freezing facility is available then try to freeze clear pond water or take some melted snow to form your ice glass.

Step 2: Take a knife or any other sharp edged object to carve the ice into a convex shape i.e. thinner around the edges and thicker in the middle. Smooth the ice surface as it will give a direct, focused, and saturated beam on your tinder. Your hands are the best tools to smooth the surface of ice as the temperature of your hands will melt the ice to the extent and shape as required.

Step 3: Angle the ice block just like a magnifying glass and put consistent focus on the tinder nest until you create fire from ice.

Chapter 5 – Ready to use Methods

These days everything is automated, convenient, and electrical and so is fire. The knowledge and skill of old school primitive methods is fine, but those applications of these methods require time and energy that people born in this century or the last two decades of the last one do not usually have – and no, please don't blame the climatic changes once again. We need everything quick and readily available from food to fire, so here are few tips.

5.1 Magnesium Strip

Find this wonder box in the picnic and adventure section of a superstore or find it online. It works fast and amazing and has a very convenient size to fit even in pant pockets.

It is small bar shaped, dark colored set of strips with magnesium deposit on one side and a ferrocerium (flint) rod on the other side.

Step 1: Sprinkle the magnesium on tinder by scraping it with the wrong side of a knife or any other sharp edged tool. When you rub the knife on the magnesium side of the bar it will cut into small pieces and you just need to collect them on tinder.

Step 2: Now, flip the rod and file the flint rod with the spine of the knife by shaving it downward. When the metal strikes with flint, the friction will create sparks which just need to reach the magnesium powder you placed in the tinder. Magnesium is highly inflammable and it will light the tinder the moment the spark created by flint touches it.

To be more cautious, keep the knife in a stationary position and move the magnesium and flint sides of the bar on the knife in friction mode. This will protect from any unforeseen injury that may be caused if you hit yourself with the sharp edge of the knife. Many ready to use magnesium bars also come with safe blades that can be used for this purpose only and we can minus the use of the knife for this method if you have gotten hold of a magnesium strip with blade.

5.2 Survival Bracelets

Survival bracelets are commonly used in military purposes by troops deployed in difficult areas. These are almost complete kits with tools ranging from whistles to navigators that are all managed in one light weighted bracelet. Survival bracelets are catching more attention due to their durability and usability, however, the cost of these bracelets tend to be on the higher side when compared to other methods described in this book.

These complete tool kits may include a compass, ropes, watch, GPS, flint, or magnesium based fire starter depending on its type, brand, and utility. Some survival bracelets even include mechanical flint striker lighters which work on the same mechanics as that of conventional metal based lighters that include ferrocerium and/or magnesium.

Chapter 6 – Things to Remember

Having the skills and tools to start a fire by yourself without a match or lighter is equally important to remembering a few important factors which can bolster your ability to start fire in the least possible time and energy consuming manner. Success of an emergency fire comes with a set of frameworks which require mental stability and the ability to think straight at the top. The tools, methods, techniques, and below listed requirements are secondary to being in right frame of mind.

Go through the details explained in each subsection below to understand what complement the above methods and techniques, and what settings are mandatory to start a perfect fire in the wilderness.

6.1 Fire bed and its location

Choose a dry and flat surface to prepare your fire bed. Fire can be your friend one moment and enemy another, so select your fire bed location wisely to assure that the bushes, trees, or your tent close to the burning area do not catch fire. A dry surface will help you ignite fire rapidly and your tinder will work as a more efficient and consumable fuel. If it is a camp fire or a fire to light the surroundings of your camp while you sleep tight inside then make it wind protected. Prepare the fire bed with help of fuel tinder and kindle fuel around the area which is not directly exposed to wind. This can extinguish your fire. For an ideal fire site, dig a pit roughly 6 inches deep and place your firewood inside it for the sake of preparing a fire bed. Make sure that the pit is flat, clear of bushes and any wet objects, and then place small rocks around the verge of this pit. Having a deep fire bed surrounded by relatively bigger rocks will not only resist wind from reaching the fire, but also help restraining coal and ashes within the pit. It is given that you have already taken care of water before leaving home, but it is even better if the fire point is close to a source of ample water to use it to diffuse fire as and when needed.

6.2 Tinder

You can chose tinder from a variety of options available - not obviously driven by your own likeness in the survival, but the situation and your surroundings. Try looking for something which is completely dry, soft, and easy to handle. Scrape some skin from the trunks of trees, get hold of some lint, add some bird feathers if you can find them, collect dry leaves, take out some cotton balls, or put some pine needles and papers in your backpack. It is a great added advantage if you are in possession of a knife or can access one in emergency situations. This does not only help you cut and shave firewood and tree branches from sources, but also enable you to carve out and trim different objects that you would need in applying different methods of starting a fire.

6.3 Fuel

A fire bed is prepared with large, stiff, and multilayered branches of trees or pieces of wood. This is the main fuel of fire which is going to decide the warmth of the fire as well as its persistence and resistance to interruptions, like wind. The list of woods to select from to prepare fire bed fuel is also very long. Birch trees, spruce, oak, and beech are good choices for a long, stable, and warm fire. Collect as much fuel as you believe is sufficient and place pieces or branches of fuel one over another. Then move them deeper into the fire from time to time to make sure that each piece is burnt and consumed till the end. It is better to use branches and pieces of wood which are bigger than 1 foot in size.

6.4 Safety

Safety is important and in cases where you are packing for adventure trips, it is advisable to carry ready to use tools for creating fire as they are arguably safer, more convenient, and more human friendly alternatives to methods that old folks used to follow. When the fire is needed immediately and it is crucial then do not wait for rescue and get hold of things you need to get, in your mind, to start fire. Take care while working with knives, spindles, or while shaving trees for tinder and breaking branches for fuel. Instead of using your knee or elbow power to detach a branch of tree, always look for ways that can release physical pressure from you and decrease chances of injury.

Conclusion

Setting up fire is a tricky, tedious, and dangerous venture when it is done away from the typical facilities and instruments made for this purpose that also come with complete safety measures. However, with the knowledge of methods, materials to use, mechanics, and a little common sense, one can ignite the flames using unconventional techniques in unforeseen circumstances. Prior to this, the primary knowledge of fire, its composition, and the environment that supports it is equally important. So, take these steps and you will be prepared to start a fire in most situations. Remember though, to use caution and always find the easiest ways to complete these tasks.

Author Bio

Muhammad Usman is a distinguished medical graduate of Allama Iqbal medical college (AIMC). He is a professional writer who has been in the field for more than 4 years. During this time he has produced 10,000+ articles, blogs and eBooks on various niches related to diseases, health, fitness, nutrition and well-being. He is a regular contributor to several journals related to medicine and surgery. He is the editor of several journals and newspapers.

Check out some of the other JD-Biz Publishing books

Gardening Series on Amazon

Health Learning Series

How to Start A Fire in a Survival Situation

Country Life Books

Health Learning Series

- Amazing Health Benefits of Intermittent Fasting
- What Makes Me Fat? How to eliminate obesity naturally!
- Natural Cures of Anxiety
- Medical Conditions Requiring Paleo Diet
- How to Eliminate Heart Burn and Acid Reflux Naturally
- Eliminate Pain! How to get rid of arthritis and joint pain naturally!
- Ways to Improve Self-Esteem
- How to Avoid Brain Aging Dementia - Memory Loss Naturally
- Paleo Diet Side Effects
- Paleo Diet Good or Bad? An Analysis of Arguments and Counter-Arguments
- How to Get Rid of High Blood Pressure or Hypertension Naturally
- Health Benefits of Meditation
- Paleo Diet For Weight Loss
- Paleo Diet for Athletes
- How to Reduce the Chances of a Heart Attack
- How to Get Rid of Asthma Naturally

Amazing Animal Book Series

Learn To Draw Series

How to Build and Plan Books

Entrepreneur Book Series

Our books are available at

1. Amazon.com
2. Barnes and Noble
3. Itunes
4. Kobo
5. Smashwords
6. Google Play Books

Publisher

JD-Biz Corp

P O Box 374

Mendon, Utah 84325

http://www.jd-biz.com/

Printed in Great Britain
by Amazon